WHERE WE GATHER

WE GATHER AT AN ISLAMIC MOSQUE

A Place in Our Community

by Golriz Golkar

PEBBLE
a capstone imprint

Published by Pebble, an imprint of Capstone
1710 Roe Crest Drive, North Mankato, Minnesota 56003
capstonepub.com

Copyright © 2026 by Pebble, a Capstone imprint. All rights reserved. No part of this publication may be reproduced in whole or in part, or stored in a retrieval system, or transmitted in any form or by any means, electronic, mechanical, photocopying, recording, or otherwise, without written permission of the publisher.

Library of Congress Cataloging-in-Publication Data is available on the Library of Congress website.
9798875223167 (hardcover)
9798875223112 (paperback)
9798875223129 (ebook PDF)

Editorial Credits
Designer: Sarah Bennett; Media Researchers: Svetlana Zhurkin and Jo Miller; Production Specialist: Tori Abraham

Image Credits
Getty Images: AnthonyRosenberg, cover, Photographed by MR.ANUJAK JAIMOOK, 11; Shutterstock: Alexey Pavlishak, 8, Anton Starikov, 20, evipanda, 4, ImageBank4u, 6, Indra_aldyla, 19, InveStock, 16, kizuuuneko, design element (throughout), Magic Orb Studio, 18, Melnikov Dmitriy, 14, Neeyaa, 9, Nick N A, 5, Petr Bonek, 7, Sener Dagasan, 13, surendra, 17, TonyV3112, 15, Yulia_B, 12, ZAINUDHEEN KAPPAN, 10

Any additional websites and resources referenced in this book are not maintained, authorized, or sponsored by Capstone. All product and company names are trademarks™ or registered® trademarks of their respective holders.

Printed and bound in China. 6274

Table of Contents

What Is a Mosque? 4

Going to a Mosque 8

Exploring a Mosque 10

Mosques and the Community 16

Make a Mosque 20

Glossary 22

Read More 23

Internet Sites 23

Index... 24

About the Author 24

Words in **bold** are in the glossary.

What Is a Mosque?

More than 1.9 billion Muslim people live around the world. They follow a religion called Islam. They pray in a building called a mosque.

Families gather to pray at a mosque.

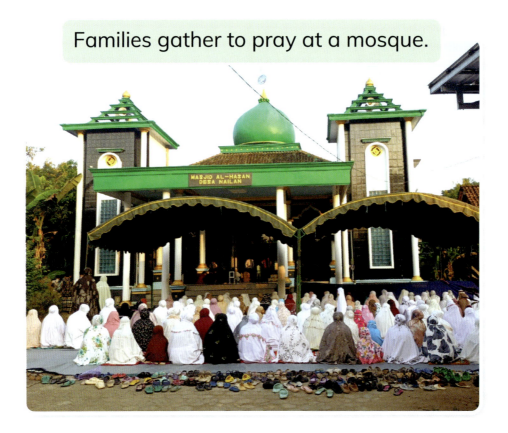

The Blue Mosque in Turkey was built in the early 1600s.

Some mosques are small. Muslims in the community gather there. Other cities have big mosques. Thousands of people visit. They may come from far away.

5

Minarets can be hundreds of feet tall.

Big mosques may have golden decorations. There are big domes on top. Tall towers called minarets are often built nearby. The word *minaret* means "**beacon**."

A person called a crier or a **muezzin** stands in the towers. The muezzin calls out to Muslims at prayer times.

Muezzins are chosen for their clear voices.

Going to a Mosque

Many mosques are open all day. People visit when they like. Most Muslims go on Fridays. They join group prayers at noon. A leader called an imam gives a **sermon**.

Many Muslims pray five times a day.

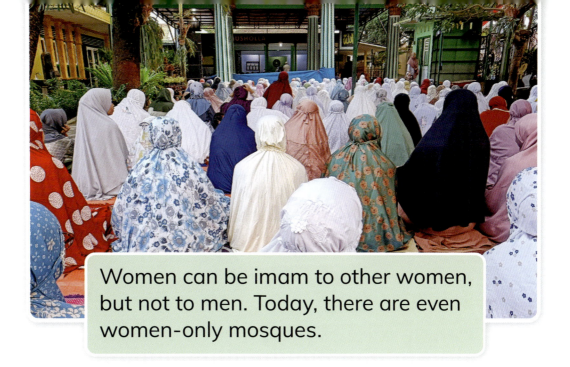

Women can be imam to other women, but not to men. Today, there are even women-only mosques.

Weddings and funerals are also times for gathering and prayers at the mosque. Muslim couples say special prayers when they marry. Muslims also gather to pray at funerals.

Men and women have their own spaces. Some mosques have special areas for children. Visitors who are not Muslim can visit too. They pray with everyone else.

Exploring a Mosque

The entrance of a mosque has a washing area. In large mosques, there may be faucets in the wall. In smaller mosques, people just use the restrooms.

People take off their shoes. They wash their faces, arms, and feet.

Some mosques have pools of water for washing.

Prayer rooms are peaceful places.

They enter a large and open space. This is the prayer room. There are no chairs. Instead, the floor may be covered with rugs.

One wall has a small opening. It is called a mihrab. It marks the direction of Mecca in Saudi Arabia. Mecca is the holiest city.

Mihrabs are small but elaborate spaces.

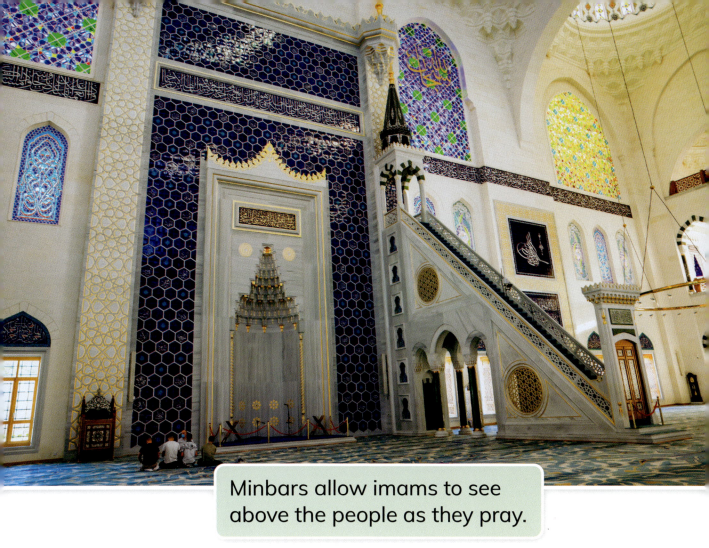

Minbars allow imams to see above the people as they pray.

Muslims stand or kneel in the prayer room. They face the mihrab. A small tower is on the right. It is called a minbar. This is where the imam gives sermons.

Green, blue, white, black, and gold are the holy colors of Islam.

Mosques have no pictures or statues. Instead, they are often decorated with **mosaics**. The tiles are bright and colorful.

The special lettering used to write the Koran is called calligraphy.

Sometimes there is writing on the walls. They are words from the Muslim **holy** book, the Koran.

15

Mosques and the Community

Mosques are places to listen and learn. In the past, rulers used mosques as meeting places. Schools and libraries were close by.

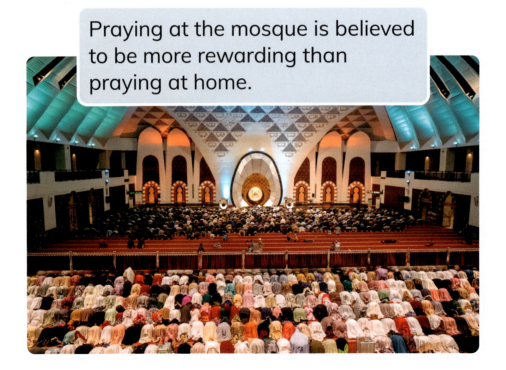

Praying at the mosque is believed to be more rewarding than praying at home.

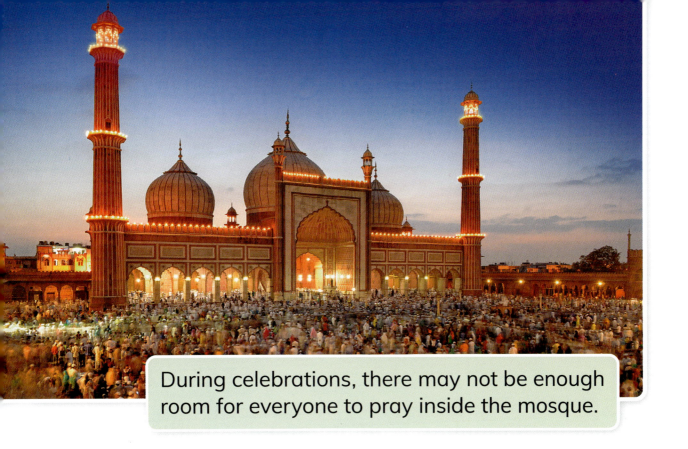

During celebrations, there may not be enough room for everyone to pray inside the mosque.

Mosques today are mostly prayer houses. They are also meeting places during special Muslim holidays. Muslims visit mosques during the holy month of **Ramadan**.

Thousands of people gather at large mosques. They pray and listen to sermons.

Mosques may have a small school. Students can learn about the Koran there.

Special community events bring Muslims together. People from other religions are included too. Different **traditions** are celebrated.

Book rests called rehals hold copies of the Koran during study.

Mosque schools are called madrasas.

Mosques bring Muslims together in prayer. They are also community centers. People help each other. They teach and learn. Have you ever been inside a mosque?

19

Make a Mosque

What You Need:

- shoebox without a lid
- colorful construction paper
- glue stick
- scissors
- markers
- pencil

What You Do:

1. Cover the outside of the shoebox in construction paper. Use glue to hold the paper in place.
2. Give your mosque an entrance. With an adult's help, cut a small, rounded door in the box. It should be in the middle of one of the long sides.

3. Cut two half-circles out of the construction paper. Glue one directly above the door you made. The straight edge of the half-circle should be near the top edge of the box with the round part pointing up.

4. Repeat on the other long side of the box. Now your mosque has a dome!

5. Cut out four tall rectangles. Trim one end of each rectangle to make a point. Glue a tower at each corner of the mosque.

6. Decorate the inside of the mosque. Start with the washing area. Then, move to the prayer room. Cut out small paper rectangles to make rugs. Decorate them with markers.

7. Use markers or bits of construction paper to make mosaics on the walls.

Glossary

beacon (BEE-kuhn)—a signal that guides or affects others in a positive way

holy (HO-lee)—related to a higher power

mosaic (mo-ZAY-ik)—a decoration made with colored materials that make pictures or patterns

muezzin (moo-EZZ-uhn)—a person who calls the faithful to prayer at an Islamic mosque

Ramadan (RAH-muh-dahn)—the ninth month of the Islamic calendar which is called a holy month; most Muslims fast during this time

sermon (SUR-muhn)—a speech made by a religious leader

tradition (truh-DIH-shun)—a belief, idea, or practice passed down from one generation to another

Read More

Andrews, Elizabeth. *Islam*. Minneapolis: DiscoverRoo, an imprint of Pop!, 2024.

Gutta, Razeena Omar. *Zamzam for Everyone: Sharing Water at Hajj*. Concord, MA: Barefoot Books, 2024.

Khan, Ausma Zehanat. *Ramadan: The Holy Month of Fasting*. Custer, WA: Orca Book Publishers, 2025.

Internet Sites

BBC: A Visit to a Mosque
bbc.co.uk/bitesize/articles/zfwphcw

National Geographic Kids: Celebrating Ramadan
kids.nationalgeographic.com/history/article
/ramadan

Ramadan: Be Good to Yourself and to Others
cbc.ca/kids/articles/ramadan-be-good
-to-yourself-and-to-others

Index

funerals, 9

imams, 8, 9, 13

Koran, 15, 18

marriages, 9

mihrabs, 12, 13

minarets, 6

minbars, 13

mosaics, 14, 21

muezzins, 7

prayer, 4, 7, 8, 9, 11, 13, 16, 17, 19, 21, 22

Ramadan, 17, 22, 23

washing areas, 10, 21

About the Author

Golriz Golkar has written more than 100 nonfiction and fiction books for children. Inspired by her work as an elementary school teacher, she loves to write the kinds of books that students are excited to read. Golriz lives in France with her husband and young daughter. She thinks children are the very best teachers, and she loves learning from her daughter every day.